SCENARIOS OF

LOVE

FROM A POET'S PEN

DEDICATION

To My Parents
Bobbie J. Asbury and the late Willie Asbury

My Sisters
Brenda Carr, Cynthia Asbury

My Brother-In-Law
Harold Carr

My Niece
Khalilah S. Asbury

My Great niece
Ava T. Irving

My Little People
Kelci A. Northcutt, David T. Northcutt, Kaitlyn A. Northcutt, Dylan T. Northcutt, Dustin T. Northcutt, Malaysia A. Gaskin, Jaysen Beverly, Troy Beverly, Billy Peele Jr., Brianna Mosely, Kandis Parks, Kassidy J. Leonard, Bryana C. Dunn, Loren Dunn, Londyn Dunn, Lorenzo Dunn Jr., Lyrik Dunn, Justin Howard, Jordyn Howard

<u>CONTENTS</u>

CHAPTER 1: YOUNG AND IN LOVE

CHAPTER 2: IF ONLY YOU KNEW

CHAPTER 3: I'M SO INTO YOU

ABOUT THE AUTHOR

ACKNOWLEDGMENTS

To my family and friends and those of you who have continuously encouraged me, believed in me and challenged me to share my words and thoughts with the world, I Thank You!

I won't list names this time for fear of leaving someone out, but I believe you know who you are. Again, I thank you!

Love…everybody wants it, everybody needs it, every-
body desires it
We have our own ideas of what love is
What it feels like, what it looks like, how it smells, how
it tastes

We write songs about it, dream about it, can't wait to
give love, see love, hear love, receive love, we just
want…love

In the name of love, I present to you a few
Scenarios of Love From A Poet's Pen

I hope you will enjoy.

Love ya!

CHAPTER 1
YOUNG AND IN LOVE

Alfreda Asbury

ME AND YOU

I heard a song
I saw your smile
So warm, so tender
To you my love
I think I'll surrender
To you I'll trust
My deepest hopes and fears
We'll share dreams, promises, secrets
Pain, sorrow and tears
We'll laugh, play, joke and cry
Sure we'll also fuss, but we'll get by
Understanding each other, friends and lovers too
That's how it's gonna be, just me and you

ONE KISS

One kiss was all it took,
and again I find myself falling for you.
Getting hooked!
I think that I'm over you,
but at times like these
I don't know what to do?
I don't want to get caught up
in the dreams I like to make.
But when you do things like this,
it's so hard for me to take.

"No, no, not again", my mind always says!
Then my heart steps in and takes control,
and things don't go my way.
I know that I can't have you,
but what am I to do?

You don't realize, that again,
here I am falling for you.
Time comes and time goes,
without you on my mind.
Then I happen to see you,
it happens all the time.

"No, no, not again", my mind always says!
Then my heart steps in and takes control,
and things don't go my way.
I know that I can't have you,
but what am I to do?

SPEND TIME WITH ME

Sit with me,
as I watch the sun rise.
I want to see your love for me
as I look into your eyes.

Talk with me,
throughout the course of the day.
I'm very much interested
in the things you have to say.

Dine with me,
by music and candlelight.
The mood has been set,
it's a beautiful night.

Dance with me,
as the day comes to an end.
Hold me close, tighter,
don't let this moment end.

Lay with me,
keep me safe and warm.
Let's drift off to sleep
lying in each other's arms.

THE MEETING AT THE PARTY

The music was playing,
thumping and pumping real loud.
She was shaking her booty
when she saw him in the crowd.
She did some fancy steps
hoping he'd catch her stare,
but after a couple of wild spins
she looked up and he was no longer there.
She tried to see if he went to the other side,
and that's when the DJ decided it was
time to do the electric slide.
She made her way quickly off the floor
not in a jamming mood anymore.
She had to find him, and if she did, what would she
say?
What had come over her to make her feel this way?
Something told her she just had to meet this man.
And as if it was by magic, someone reached out and
grabbed her by the hand.
It felt like an eternity as she slowly turned around,
but when she did, she was glad at what she'd found.
For there he stood, tall, dark, muscular and looking
very, very good.
Then he asked her to dance knowing that she would.
"What's your name?" She heard him say.
While leading her to the dance floor where she was
sure they'd dance the night away.

NO PROMISES

Promise me, no promises
I've been through it all before.
Things said, but never done
I don't want to hear it anymore.
Now's the beginning of something
that is special and new.
Promise me, no promises
just let me love you.
Nothing's guaranteed in this world
and this I truly know.
So why not take our time and
give love a chance to grow.
Promise me, no promises
let's just do our best.
That's all I ask of you.
Love will do the rest.

TOUGH

Refusing to crack.
Yeah, that's me,
solid as a brick.
Big, bad and bold,
check out my tricks.
Tell 'em, "what you say?"
Aww, alright, ok.
I'll confess if I must.
When it gets right down to it,
I'm really not that tough.

SEASONAL LOVE

Your love is like the winter snow
  Covering me gently as it flows

Your love is like the first day of spring
  Giving me all that one love could possibly bring

Your love is like a warm summer's breeze
  Blowing ever so softly, surrounding me

Your love is like the colors of the fall
  Red, yellow, green and brown, you give me them all

Your love is the one reason
  That I make it through all four seasons

YOUNG LOVE HEARSAY

She said he said that she told him that he said, you
said she said that he said, "he likes me".

Well I said, "that if she said he said, that she told him
that he said, you said she said that he said he likes me
then it must be true".
That's when he said that what she said, you said he
said wasn't really what he said, she said he said that
you said…"stop!"
Wait a minute everybody's saying it, but you?

Just tell me, do I stand a chance with you?

SCHOOLGIRL CRUSH

Can't explain this feeling I get when you come around.
It starts at my heart and goes all the way down.
It goes to my toes, but not before stopping by to touch
my soul... in the most tender way.

I get nervous, and as corny as it sounds, my knees get
weak.
My mouth dries up until it's hard for me to speak.
When you say, "hello", I mumble something, but what
it is one only knows.
So I just smile hoping you'll hang around for a while.

I listen intently as you laugh and talk, and even
though I hate to see you leave...
I love to watch you as you stroll away, leaving a feeling
that's hard to believe.
It's just something about a brother's walk that always
gets to me.

I just can't wait until we are together,
because we will be, watch you'll see.
I saw us in a dream last night
and we were working out alright.

That is until my mother turned on the light.
My dream was interrupted, but that's alright,
because I played it off real cool.
Knowing that tomorrow I'd be seeing you in school.

CHAPTER 2
IF ONLY YOU KNEW

SURPRISE

Come take my love and away we'll run

What if I looked into your eyes?
Would it come as a surprise
if I told you that I love you?

If I told you that
I wanted to hold you close
And never ever let you go.
Would it come as a surprise?

If I said, "come take my hand".
Would you finally understand or
would it come as a surprise?
I have loved you for so long.
More than you'll ever know.
I just couldn't take it any more
and had to make my feelings known.
So...

If I tell you you're the one.
Does it come as a surprise?

If only I could get you to see
how you really feel about me.
Tell me what do I have to do?
Or...

Would it come as a surprise
when you finally realize
that you love me too?

CURIOSITY

Saw you there, watching me.
Wondering, what did you see?
Did you see me watching you too?
Standing here, wondering…
what am I gonna do?
If you should smile, come over and sit awhile.
I wish you'd hurry up and speak,
'cause my knees are getting awfully weak.

YOU

You,
  are my weakness
  even though you are unaware of the power you hold

You,
  are my strength
  giving me the power to keep the feelings under control

You,
  are totally oblivious
  of the confusion you have caused me to feel

You,
  are directly responsible
  for the soreness of my openness that slowly tries to
  heal

You,
  are the reason that allows me to dream, but,

You,
  are like me, unable to see what they mean

WINDOW OF MY HEART

Peeping out from the window of my heart
Afraid to open the door and let the feeling start

Scared of what exposing my feelings might do to me
Afraid of the person I may come to be

If I open my heart and soul to you…
once they're in your care, will you know what to do?

My heart and feelings are very tender things
And I'm always wary of the pain that love often brings

So I must decide if I should take a chance
And open the door of my heart to a new romance

Or should I keep my distance and keep you far apart
Looking at you only through the window of my heart

MY IMAGINATION

Can I pretend for just a moment
that you belong to me?

Would it be awfully wrong
for me to engage in this brief fantasy?

I can't help feeling this feeling that I feel
so forgive me for a moment

While I pretend it's real
Imagining that you really care,
for me

Even though you're totally unaware
of what it is you do to me.
You just don't see, so
can I pretend for just awhile?
It's meant for me, your beautiful smile

REGRETS

I never told you
Never provided a real clue.
But, I wish I
Would've, Could've, Should've
had the nerve to let you know.
Had the guts to tell you so.

I never made a move.
Never got into the groove
But, I wish I
Could've, Should've, Would've
taken a chance and
invited you to my dance.

I never said a word
How I felt, you never heard.
But, I wish, I
Should've, Would've, Could've
put a whisper in your ear
of my desire to have you near.

But, I didn't!

Now, I wish, I
Would've been very brave…
Could've been more bold…
Should've had the courage.
But, instead I have regrets,
because I never told you
but I Should've, Would've… if I Could've!

CHAPTER 3
I'M SO INTO YOU

ONLY A MINUTE

If only for a minute, when you hold me
all my troubles of the day...
The worries and problems seem to fade away

For a moment my world is at peace
All of my cares seem to cease
If only for a minute when you hold me
I feel safe in your arms, secure from any harm

And that's how it should be
If only for a minute
When you hold me
I can let my worries go
It's all because you make it so
And baby I just want you to know
If only for a minute when you hold me

THE RIDE

I hold onto you tightly
As we rock back and forth
slightly,
perfectly.
In tune to each other's syncopated rhythm
we enjoy the ride
With my arms locked around your waist
I bury my head in your back
Intoxicated by the smell of you
I try to inhale your very breath
Oh, how I love this
as we continue to rock,
to roll, to glide
Together… you and me
On a horseback ride

THE REQUEST LINE

Hey Mr. DJ,
Play me a happy love song
A tune that I can sing
as I think of him all day long

Seems like the request line
always has the same old, sad love songs
You know, about who did what to who
and where did they go wrong

Give me a melody that I can hum for awhile
I wanna hear something that's gonna make me smile

Love's been good and love's been bad,
but I'd rather be happy in love
than in love and still sad

So please Mr. DJ,
honor my request
Put the song on
Love and me will do the rest

C'MON

Love is in the air
We've got so much to share
Let's go over there
C'mon

The lights have been dimmed
Your hair is cut and trimmed
I've got on my red dress with the short hem
C'mon

The candles are burning
Luther's CD is turning
We're both yearning
C'mon

The wine has been chilled
The table is set
This is almost as good as
it's gonna get
C'mon

It's been a long day
I'm ready to relax and play
What else can I say?
Except, Baby
C'mon

LEFTOVERS

I am tasting memories of you
We dined together last night,
and for me it has ended too soon

The candles have burned out, the music
is no longer playing softly, and
the sun has replaced the moon
you too are gone.
However, I have leftovers from the main meal,
which I am eating now

The dessert was dark, sweet, rich and full
of nuts and goodies, melt in your mouth, a
delicious chocolate - it was you

Just the memories of the evening
have made me hungry again
You'll be here soon, as I await your return

I have warmed up the leftovers
I am eating and tasting them
My memories of you
Ummmmm...

IN THE MOOD

I am in the mood
to touch and be touched
I am in the mood
to play grown

I am in the mood
to be fed, to be led
I am in the mood
to travel to destinations unknown

I am in the mood
to laugh at silly jokes
I am in the mood
to be read to, sung to

I am in the mood
to be caressed and stroked
I am in the mood
for some stimulating conversation

I am in the mood
to have a good time
I am in the mood
for some love and relaxation

I am in the mood
to rejoice in the joy that is mine
As always, I am in the mood...for you
The way you treat me, the things that you do

I am in the mood
now what are you going to do?

I'M SO INTO YOU

Didn't want to do love again
Me and my life were just moving along
Dancing to our own beat
Singing our own song

Then one day I caught your smile

There is just something about your walk
I could sit for hours
Just listening... to you talk

Your presence is so intoxicating
Just being around you is exhilarating

The way you treat me
The things you do
The way you make me feel

I'm so into you

CHAPTER 4
WHAT'S GOING ON?

THE LAST TIME

The candles have burned down low
I'm all dressed up with no place to go.

The food is cold and your excuses are old
The fire is almost gone

And here I sit, for the last time!

PHOTOGRAPHS

As I sat staring into space
There it was
right in front of my face
Begging me to come and take a look
To leaf through the pages of my picturebook

There I see snapshots of you and I
I try to fight back the tears
No, I don't want to cry,
but the sadness fills me
as I think of how it used to be

It was you and me
It was always we
And that's how it still looks
in the pages of my picturebook

As I turn the pages and see the faces
that are now part of my past
At the time, who would've imagined
that the good times with you wouldn't last

It used to be you and me
It was always we
And that's how it still looks
in the pages of my picturebook

GOING WITH THE FLOW

It was good for the moment
this I now see.

As I come to the realization
that it wasn't meant to be.

A kind of forever thing
that real love is supposed to bring.

I had doubts from the start,
didn't want to play with my heart.

But sometimes it's best you know
to just relax and go with the flow.

To take the ups and downs all in stride,
because you know it's going to be
a short and exciting ride.

Well now it has come to an end...
time to get off and wait for
the next one to begin.

Yes, it was good for the moment
this I now know.

Sometimes it's not all that bad
to just go with the flow.

I SURRENDER

Giving up on love
not because I want to
It just seems that it's
the easiest thing to do

REFLECTIONS

In the morning
In the mirror
How do you face yourself?
Knowing that last night
while I lay here alone
you were laying with someone else

In the morning
In the mirror
Tell me what do you see?
Did I ever cross your mind?
Did you even think about me?

In the morning
In the mirror
In the light of day
As you look into your eyes
to yourself, exactly what do you say?

LETTING GO

I finally realized
when I looked into your eyes
that I've got to let go.

It breaks my heart,
but it's the right thing,
I know.

There comes a point where
one must choose which way to go.

It's just a fact of life
that can hurt one so bad.
It's sad, I know, but it's true.
No matter what my heart says, I've got
to let go of you.

The memories will linger on, I'm sure
'cause I suspect for that there is
no real cure.

Don't hold me back, please just let me go.
Because, I finally know
that the best thing to do for us
is for *me* to let you go.

BACK TRACK

Driving through the park,
taking the path we used to go.
Saw our favorite little statue,
it just doesn't seem so.

Thinking of the time when love was all I knew.
The love that you had for me and me for you.

Going back wasn't easy,
but it was something I had to do.
Just had to figure out
how in the world did I lose you?

Oh, how it hurt so bad inside.
To go back where love was born,
to find out how it died.

GOODBYE

"Goodbye"
was all you said
And then all at once
The emotions began to course through my heart and
my head
What was I feeling?
I did not know
I wanted you to stay, but I could not say why
it started with goodbye.

It hasn't ended yet.
I never dreamed I could feel this way
about anyone before.
With the dawning of each day,
I just want to love you more and more.
To give you all that I can.
I don't know why
it started with goodbye.

I hope it never ends,
'cause this love I have for you
is such a good, good feeling!
And I just can't explain why, but,
this I do know…
it started with goodbye.

CHAPTER 5
ANY LOVE

ODE TO COOLEY HIGH

It was my first movie I was allowed to see
by myself, with my friends.

Since that time, I've seen it again
and again, and again and again,
and ...again.

I fell in love with
...the music, Motown
...Cochise, the coolest basketball dude around
...Preach, the aspiring poet
...Pooter, who was cool and didn't know it
...Johnny Mae, who said I'll do it if she will
...Cousin Jimmy, who scammed the white guy in
search of a thrill
...Brenda who opened Preach's nose up wide,
even loved the thugs who took them for a wild ride
...Martha ain't take no stuff in her store with her axe
and
...Mr. Mason who had the boy's backs.

After that, every time I would hear
"It's So Hard To Say Goodbye",
I'd think of the movie and it made me cry.

For it brought back memories of
my love affair with Cooley High.
Swish...for the brothers who ain't here!

BETWEEN THE BROTHERS

A hug, a smile
An open display of affection
for one another
I love to see that
Between the Brothers

Affection unabashedly shown
Understanding the pain of one another
Through a connection
others have never known, it's just
Between the Brothers

Extending out a hand
to your fellow black man
Not just because you have to,
but because you can
Between the Brothers

Knowing that together
you stand tall
your history is a great one
that amazes them all
Between the Brothers

Calling each other by
your name and not
out of your name,
because you are aware of
from whence you came
That's love
Between the Brothers

It thrills my soul and warms my heart
to know that you won't be torn apart
You were aware from the start
that it's sanctioned from above
Love, to each other
Love Between the Brothers

HE LOVED HER

She paid…
 for his car,
 his clothes,
 his room and board,
 because, *He loved Her*

She paid…
 the loans,
 the bills,
 his and hers,
 even for the thrills,
 because, He loved Her

She paid,
 the price every day
 with her friends, family
 job, and other opportunities
 that came her way,
 because, He loved Her

She paid,
 with sweat,
 blood and tears,
 heartache and pain
 over the many years,
 because, He loved Her

She paid,
 and paid, and paid,
 only to realize
 after he'd left
 that she couldn't

balance her checkbook,
because, He loved Her
and his payments were overdue

44

GOD'S LOVE

If not for His love,
I would not be.
For it's His guiding light
that helps me to see.

If not for His love,
just what would I do?
Who else could I depend on
to *always* come through?

If not for His love,
life would be a different game.
For in a world that's ever-changing
His love will remain the same.

If not for His love,
I don't know where I'd be.
For in my darkest hours
it's always been God's love that has comforted me.

NOT READY FOR GOODBYE

(In Memory Of David L. Turner)
1962-1982

As I walked through the places where we used to be,
I realize that now, it's a memory.
It seems as if it was only yesterday,
in my mind I don't think it'll ever go away.

Why did time have to fly?
Why did you have to go?

Since you left, things haven't been the same anymore.
The rooms are filled with your laughter.
The air is filled with your cheer.
The only thing that's missing is that you're not here!

Why did time have to fly?
Why did you have to leave?

It's something I've learned to accept,
it's something that had to be.
Time goes on and we must grow,
but before I can I just want to know...

Why did you have to leave?
Why did time have to fly?
Because I wasn't ready, no, not quite
to say goodbye.

WE

He was hip-hop
I was more be-bop
He was downtown
I was more uptown

He listens to Tupac, Snoop
Dr. Dre and Biggie
Was dancing along with Will
when he was gettin' jiggy

I listen to Miles, Sarah
The Temptations and Coltrane
Can remember watching Marvin
perform on Soul Train

He taught me the Bank Head Bounce
and his favorite, the Harlem Shake
I taught him how to do the hustle,
two-step, the bump and even the snake

He surfs the net, flips through the magazines
and believes everything he hears on the news
I read the paper and books, Zora, J. California Cooper
and everything by Langston Hughes

He plays video games
Likes going to the movies
And for him
a stop at Burger King will do

I like to visit museums
Go to plays and enjoy
candlelight and a
dinner for two

Obviously he and I
are from different times and places
as you and others can surely see
We can tell by the strange stares
that they wonder, together,
how did we come to be?

To most observers
we're quite a strange and unusual pair
But we no longer ask ourselves why
honestly we no longer care

We genuinely love each other
We don't care what people have to say
Oh and did I forget to mention that
I was born in December and he in May?

LOVE LIST

He was looking for love and she wanted to love him
but, he thought she was...
Too short, too tall, too dark, too light,
Whatever it was, something just wasn't right
Her hair was too short, too long
She was too skinny, too thick, too fat
It was always this, the other, or that
She was too needy, too greedy
She had a daughter, she had a son
For many reasons she just wasn't the one
He didn't like the way she looked when she walked
The way she sounded when she talked
It was just so much wrong... so he just sat alone
Reviewing his requirement list for love
And she knew this because...

She was looking for love and he wanted to love her
But, she thought he was...
Too short, too tall, too dark, too light
Whatever it was, something just wasn't right
His hair was too short, he wore braids, he had a'fro, he
was bald
Just too many wrongs to name them all
He was too skinny, too stocky, too fat
It was always this, the other, or that
He had a daughter, he had a son
For many reasons, he just wasn't the one
He didn't wear a suit and tie, his shoes weren't right
The pants he wore were just too high and just too tight
The car he drove was all wrong, so she just sat alone
Reviewing her requirement list for love
And he knew this because...

He was looking for love and he wanted to love her
She was looking for love and she wanted to love him
But...

50

YOU CAME TO ME

You came to me
Heart in your hand
With promises of a love
that was unconditional and pure

My acceptance wasn't immediate
My belief in your declaration
a little unsure

I didn't believe it was true
Almost dismissed your heart and you

But then love stepped in
Convinced me it was time to begin
To try, to trust
Love made me see
that this truly
was meant to be
Because with your heart in your hand
You came to me

CHAPTER 6
TREASURE

EASY

It was so easy to love you
I mean what else could I do
Your beautiful smile
Your warm and caring ways
Your thoughtfulness that brightens up my days
What can I say
It's all of the little things you do
The simple pleasures that keep me in love with you
The massaging of my feet
after a long day and I'm beat
The way you massage my scalp while you're washing
my hair
And whenever I need you to be by my side
you try your best to be there
It was so easy to love you
I mean what else could I do?
The way you go about pleasing me
The depth of your understanding and love
could compete with any sea
The gift of a single flower, a one-minute call
I believe that truly says it all
It explains it through and through
It was so easy to love you

WAITING FOR ME

I'd searched so long
to find a love like yours
For a while it seemed that
love had closed its doors on me
I couldn't understand, I wondered was it fate
then you came along and I found that

It was worth the wait
I can see that now
I'm glad you found me
to show me how, good
it could be, you loving me
And now I believe it was because
you were waiting for me

I often wondered where I'd gone wrong
What was the reason I had to wait so long
for the love that was meant for me?
I'm glad I waited 'cause I believe

It was worth the wait
I can see that now
I'm glad you found me
to show me how, good
it could be, you loving me
And now I believe we were meant to be
'cause you were waiting for me

WE LOVE

We love soft…
We love hard…
We love long…
We love strong!

We love too much…
We love not enough…
We love right…
We love wrong!
We love just because…
We love.

We love thru the joys…
We love thru the pain…
We love to the end then we

STOP!

Only to love all over again…

WELCOME

I believe I'm ready to receive
the love I know I'm worthy of

Yes, I'm ready
My heart is now steady
And I can feel that
At last this is for real

I stand here waiting
Anxiously anticipating
The joy I knew could be mine
It was only a matter of time
Love can be real
Finally, from my past I've healed
I'm ready to explore
all that love has in store for me

Now I clearly see
what is meant to be
Yes, I'm free to love you
What you are to me is all
I've ever needed love to be

Welcome

STILL HOLDING HANDS

It has been quite some time now
since we first met
We knew then that together
we'd share a journey that
we would never forget

You asked me if you
could hold my hand
And as we walked and talked
we started right then to
begin making our together plans

Then came the day
that you asked for my hand
With promises of forever
we pledged our love to each other,
and our lives together began

It only got better
I was there for you, you were there for me
You held my hand through the pain
as the cries of new life came,
and we became a family

As it is with life
The trials and tribulations
came to present themselves
We've shared everything
no matter how big or small
With love, patience and understanding
together we've weathered them all

As the sun begins a slow set
On what we've done and
who we've come to be
I'm glad we were able to follow our plans,
but more importantly, I'm glad that
we're still holding hands

ABOUT THE AUTHOR

Alfreda Asbury has been writing poetry for as long as she can remember. There is something about seeing words, thoughts and stories come together that is exciting to her, and she believes that it is her gift from God. She loves to read; her father was a voracious reader and it is from him that she inherited her love and passion for reading. Books are truly a friend of hers.

She has long shared her poetry and writings with family and friends and is excited to publish the first of what she hopes will be several poetry books. She gets her inspiration for her poems from life's daily conversations, world events, and life experiences (her own and others).

Poet Langston Hughes holds a special place in her heart. In addition, she is inspired by Maya Angelou, James Baldwin, Susan Taylor, Nikki Giovanni, Zora Neale Hurston and J. California Cooper, just to name a few. She is a native of Philadelphia, PA and currently lives in Atlanta, GA.